THE UNAUTHORISED
Corb
Bleu
Inside out

Piccadilly Press • London

meet

CORBIN BLEU

Surely Corbin Bleu is the coolest guy on the planet? He's an actor, singer, dancer and model who's been performing since he was a toddler. He's been the lead in blockbuster movies like *High School Musical* and top US TV shows like *Flight 29 Down*, become a hugely popular recording artist, graced the covers of hundreds of magazines, performed on sell-out tours across the world and is adored by millions of fans – all by the age of 18!

But success hasn't just landed in Corbin's lap. Yes, he's always been gorgeous and mega-talented, but he's worked extremely hard – from as soon as he could walk and talk! He's risen to every challenge with drive and determination, and hasn't let difficulties or knock-backs put him off his passion for performing. Corbin has given 110% to everything he has done – and continues to do so.

You might think that fame would have gone to Corbin's head. But far from it. People who know him well say he is very down-to-earth, with a great ability to laugh at himself. Corbin says,

Fast Fact!

Corbin's dad, David, quickly became an in-demand actor who has since had a very busy and successful career – you may have seen him in TV shows such as *Charmed* and *Buffy the Vampire Slayer*, and films such as *Poseidon*.

4

'You name a show business faux pas and it has happened to me – from pants with the zipper down on the red carpet, to having hair that looked like I put my finger in a light socket!' Fans who have met Corbin think he is very warm, friendly and approachable. He describes himself as, 'a very outgoing person. I'm always happy. I'm one of those people who are always smiling. If somebody described me to somebody else, they'd say "the kid with the curly hair with the big smile on his face". I get along with everybody.'

   Want to find out more about the person behind the super-funky hair and the oh-so-cute smile? For instance, was Corbin good at school? What was his very first acting break? What sort of girls does he like? What hopes and dreams does he have for the future? For the answers to these and many other essential questions, just read on. This book will tell you what the hugely talented young star, Corbin Bleu, is really like, inside and out.

Corbin's Top Tips

Here's how Corbin achieves his trademark crazy curls:
Wash, condition, comb through with a wide-toothed comb while conditioner is still in, then rinse.
Bend over and shake (looking something like a wet dog).
Apply a small amount of anti-frizz cream
(being careful not to disturb the curls!).
Bend over and shake again
(trying not to get a headache).
Voilà!

CORBIN FACT FILE

Stage name: Corbin Bleu

Real name: Corbin Bleu Reivers

Nickname: Bleuman

Birthday: 21 February 1989

Birthplace: Brooklyn, New York

Height: 5 foot 7 inches

Eyes: Brown

Hair: Who doesn't know about Corbin's hair? It's curl-tastic!

Parents: Martha Reivers (née Callari) and David Reivers

Siblings: Corbin has three younger sisters: Hunter, Phoenix and Jag

Home: Los Angeles, California, USA

Pets: None. (Corbin once explained to teenmusic.com: *'A house of six is crazy enough as it is!'*)

Fast Fact!

Corbin's star sign is Pisces. Pisces people are meant to be creative, artistic, imaginative, sensitive and romantic. Sound like Corbin?

Surrounded by Support

Corbin was part of a big, close-knit family. His mum grew up in Brooklyn with her parents and six siblings. His dad had been born in the Caribbean but his family had moved to Coney Island, New York when Corbin's dad was ten. So Corbin had two sets of grandparents, lots of aunts and uncles, and crowds of cousins living close by. His home was always full of family and friends, love and laughter.

Rooted in Show Business

Corbin Bleu was born into the world of show business.

    His mum and dad lived in the Brooklyn area of New York City. New York is packed with plays, shows, concerts and performers because the city is home to an important theatre district called Broadway. His parents are both actors. Corbin's mum also has a talent for dancing. She trained at the New York City High School of Performing Arts – a very well-known theatre school which has educated many famous performers, such as *Friends* star Jennifer Aniston and movie star Wesley Snipes. The school was also the inspiration behind the Eighties' movie and TV series *Fame*. Martha met Corbin's dad when they were both waiting around at an audition for parts in a film.

Corbin xx

7

Into the Spotlight

As a toddler, Corbin was fascinated by his dad's job. He often saw his dad on TV in commercials or guest-starring in shows, and he loved watching his dad learn his lines and rehearse. At just two years old, Corbin began copying his dad – he would memorise the lines of TV shows and films, then perform them out loud to whoever would listen.

Other people might have called Corbin a show-off, but David and Martha were thrilled that their son was clearly a born performer. Corbin's parents helped him learn acting skills, like working out the best way to deliver a line – although they found Corbin was often a natural and knew things instinctively. Corbin's parents took him for auditions for TV adverts and soon he was appearing in commercials for products like Life cereal, Bounty kitchen towels, Hasbro toys and Nabisco biscuits.

Fast Fact!

Corbin's mother is Italian-American. His father is Jamaican-American. Corbin once wrote in his online journal at corbinbleu.com that his multi-racial heritage is 'a spicy blend'.

Time Out

For Corbin, learning to act and performing in commercials wasn't work – it was just fun. But he did lots of other enjoyable things too. He loved to read books, especially if the stories were funny. And as with big families, there were always get-togethers and birthday parties and weddings to go to, trips out to restaurants or on picnics, and special treats like going out in early December to see the enormous Christmas tree put up each year at Rockefeller Center. There were holidays too, such as when Corbin was three, and his parents took him to the island of Jamaica, in the Caribbean, to visit more of his relations on his dad's side of the family.

Corbin's Top Tips

One of the first things Corbin's dad taught him was that a good actor should spend lots of time listening and watching other people. It's important to learn how to be natural rather than to try to 'act'.

Striking a Pose

Back in New York, Corbin showed such promise as a child model that he caught the eye of the Ford Modelling Agency, one of the leading model agencies in the city. It has represented many, many famous people including *Friends* star Courteney Cox-Arquette, *The OC* star Mischa Barton, and film stars Kirsten Dunst and Lindsay Lohan. Ford signed up Corbin at the age of four, and he was soon appearing in adverts for famous American clothes shops such as Gap, Macy's and Target. He was seen modelling fashions on the pages of glossy magazines called *Parenting, Child* and *American Baby*. Corbin's beaming smile also appeared on the packaging of toys and games for Toys R Us.

 CORBIN *Quick Quiz*

Q) When Corbin was four years old, his little sister Hunter came along. His parents went on to have two more girls. Can you remember their names?

A) Phoenix and Jaz

A chance to dance

Corbin didn't just stand out in auditions, he also stood out in his class at his local pre-school – for being too energetic! Corbin could never sit still and used to talk non-stop, in a very loud, lively voice. He was always bouncing about and jumping off things and chattering, yelling, singing and chuckling. He used to drive his teachers crazy!

Corbin's parents gave their son an outlet for all his energy by enrolling him in dance classes. Corbin began learning ballet and jazz. He absolutely loved it! Even though he was usually the only boy in a class full of little girls, this did not put him off at all.

Corbin's parents also encouraged him to try sports like basketball and Tae Kwon Do, but he didn't really take to them. It was clear that he had inherited his mum's talent for dancing. He had also found a passion – which has stayed with him all his life.

Corbin Hits the Stage

At the age of six, Corbin landed a part in a professional play called *Tiny Tim is Dead*. The play was a serious, upsetting one about down-and-out people living on the street. Corbin's role was especially difficult – he had to pretend to be a homeless child who could not speak. He was also the only child actor in the play, performing alongside five adults. It was a tough task but, as usual, Corbin rose to the challenge and was superb. From then on, he was truly bitten by the acting bug.

Corbin's Top Tips

Corbin's mum and dad taught him that if he failed an audition, he shouldn't take it personally and get upset – it wasn't a big deal. It happens to actors all the time and you just have to put it behind you and move on to the next thing. On the other hand, if you are successful at an audition, you shouldn't get starry-eyed and big-headed!

A Move to the Home of the Movies

In 1996, when Corbin was seven, his parents made a difficult decision. They chose to pack up and leave all their family and friends in New York and move a long way, right across the other side of the United States, to Los Angeles in California. Both Corbin's dad and Corbin needed new opportunities for their talents, and where better than the home of 'tinsel town' itself – Hollywood!

Corbin's Career Takes Off!

As seen on TV

Los Angeles leads the world when it comes to entertainment such as films, TV shows and pop music. The city is packed with studios, film sets, recording studios, production company offices, cinemas, theatres, concert venues, restaurants and clubs where stars, would-be stars, producers, directors and crew members hang-out.

With lots of new auditions on offer, Corbin's father found that he was getting more roles than ever. He had constant TV work on popular American shows including *Brooklyn South*, *Home Improvement*, *Felicity* and *Judging Amy*.

Imagine how excited Corbin must have been when he landed a recurring role in a TV series, like his father! The show was a police drama called *High Incident* and it ran for two series. It was created by Steven Spielberg, the world-famous director behind blockbuster movies such as *Jaws*, *ET*, *Raiders of the Lost Ark* and *Jurassic Park*.

The same year, Corbin was also cast in a guest role on one of the most popular TV shows ever: *ER*. He was in good company – many famous stars have had guest appearances on ER, including: Lucy Liu (from *Charlie's Angels*) and Kirsten Dunst (from *Spider-Man*). Corbin's character didn't have a name – he was credited merely as 'Little Boy'. However, he was thrilled to find himself working alongside one of the show's leads, the mega-famous George Clooney. This award-winning actor, director and producer has guest-starred on many TV shows, such as *Friends* and *South Park* and appeared as the lead

in lots of movies, including *Batman & Robin*, *Spy Kids* and *Ocean's Eleven*.
Corbin also got to spend time chatting to George Clooney when they weren't filming.
He must have felt he was one of the luckiest seven-year-olds in the world!

CORBIN
Quick Quiz

Q) 'Bleu' is the French word for blue.
Corbin's sisters also have colours for their
middle names – do you know what they are?

A) Hunter Gray, Phoenix Sage,
and Jag Sienna.

On the BIG SCREEN

Yet more exciting times were just around the corner for Corbin. In 1997, when he was just eight years old, he got his first role in a feature film. Corbin played a little boy called Johnny in a movie called *Soldier*, starring Kurt Russell, a famous actor you may have seen in *Captain Ron*, *Stargate* and *Poseidon*. Corbin's part was only small, and he wasn't instantly recognisable because his head was shaved! But he thought that acting on a huge movie set was totally fantastic, and he longed to do more.

Corbin didn't have to wait long. In 1998, as well as appearing in an episode of the TV show *Malcolm & Eddie*, Corbin won another small part in a movie. It was about surfer dudes and was called *Board Heads*. But even better was just around the corner – the following year, Corbin acted in not just one movie, but three!

Corbin played the part of a boy called Ricky in *Family Tree* – a film about a young lad who has to overcome a gang of bullies and a poor relationship with his father. The film also starred Naomi Judd, a top Country and Western singer, and it won an award at WorldFest Houston for the best independent theatrical feature film (family and children category).

Corbin also appeared in a film about low-grade superheroes, called *Mystery Men*.

He played a superhero's son called Butch. The movie featured leading Hollywood actors such as Ben Stiller (who you may know from *Night at the Museum*), William H Macy (starred in *Jurassic Park III*), and Hank Azaria (one of the main voices on *The Simpsons*).

The most successful of the three movies was a very funny film called *Galaxy Quest*, which was a spoof of popular sci-fi TV series *Star Trek*. It's about a group of actors who played the crew of a spaceship on a blockbuster TV show which has now been cancelled. A race of aliens think the washed-up actors are a real spaceship crew and rope them in to wage war on an enemy alien race who are trying to wipe them out. Corbin played the part of a genius child actor (not too much of a stretch for him) named Tommy Webber. Among the lead adult actors were movie superstars Sigourney Weaver (who starred in *Ghostbusters* and the *Alien* movies) and Alan Rickman (who starred in *Robin Hood: Prince of Thieves* and plays Professor Snape in the Harry Potter films). The film got some fantastic reviews and won a Hugo Award for Best Dramatic Presentation and two awards at the Brussels' Film Festival.

Ten-year-old Corbin must have been delighted to see his name on the credits of Hollywood movies alongside the names of some of the very best in the business!

Burn the floor

Corbin was going from strength to strength as an actor, but his first love continued to be dancing. In 2001, a multi-talented performer, Debbie Allen, opened a dance school in Los Angeles. Debbie starred as a dance teacher in the Eighties' film and TV series *Fame*. She was not just an amazing dancer, however; she was also a brilliant singer, actress, director, producer and writer. Over 500 hopefuls applied for the 150 places available at the Debbie Allen Dance Academy – Corbin was one of them, of course. His talent shone through and he was accepted straightaway.

CORBIN
Quick Quiz

Q) Corbin plays an instrument very well. Which one?

A) The piano

He embarked on a year-long course involving twelve lessons a week in all types of dance: from ballet and jazz to hip-hop and African dance. It was very intensive, but Corbin has never been afraid of hard work. He was in his element and relished every moment.

Corbin's Top Tips

Corbin explained to his high school headteacher that he thought that acting was like playing a team sport. Occasionally you take the lead, speaking a monologue, but for most of the time it's about how well you interact with others.

COOL AT SCHOOL

While busy with all his acting and dancing, Corbin had to keep up with his schoolwork too. Luckily, he is naturally very bright and eager to learn. Corbin enjoyed reading textbooks, absorbing new information and working out how to solve problems. As a result, he always got A's in every subject. Corbin did so well at school that he was put straight from the sixth grade into the eighth grade, skipping a year.

When it came to moving on to high school, Corbin knew just what he wanted. His mum had often told him great stories about her experiences at the New York City High School of Performing Arts and he longed to go to a similar type of school. So Corbin decided to try to get into the top 'fame academy' in California: the Los Angeles County High School for the Arts – known as LACHSA.

Every year, over 500 students apply to be accepted into the ninth grade (the first year), to specialise in drama, dance, music and visual arts (such as design and drawing). Competition is extremely fierce – for instance, for drama, only 40 places are available. Only the most talented applicants stand a chance. And being talented isn't enough – you have to be good at academic work too, with an average of at least a C+ across all your usual school subjects like maths, English, history and science. You have to audition in front of a panel of four judges, write an essay on why you want to attend the school and, finally, pass a daunting interview with the headteacher.

Of course, Corbin got through his audition with flying colours – his academic grades couldn't have been better, he clearly and passionately explained all his reasons for applying, and he blew away the headteacher with his confidence and maturity. Corbin was accepted!

Corbin Takes the Lead

Galaxy Quest had proved to be a very popular film and Corbin's appearance had brought him to the attention of casting directors at Fox movies. Halfway through his first year at LACHSA, Corbin had a big break – he landed his first leading role in a feature film. He was cast as the lead character of Austin in a movie called *Catch That Kid*. The film has been described as *Mission: Impossible* or James Bond for kids. It was about a twelve-year-old girl called Maddy whose dad becomes seriously ill and needs an operation that her family can't afford. She and her two best friends (one of whom was played by Corbin) get together to rob the bank where her mum works, in order to lay their hands on the necessary cash. They don't succeed – but they have a lot of excitement and adventures along the way, and everything turns out all right in the end.

The movie got some great reviews and it was nominated for a Young Artist Award for Best Feature Family Film (Drama) in 2005. Corbin had a great time working on it – not just because the plot calls for the actors to get up to all sorts of thrilling antics, but also because his co-stars, Kristen Stewart and Max Thierot, were about the same age as him and they got on very well together.

Making the movie wasn't all fun and games, however. David and Martha made a strict rule that Corbin had to do just the same schoolwork as his classmates were doing at the same time as filming. LACHSA very helpfully agreed to send Corbin all his work to do on set or at home. When he returned to high school for his second year, not only had he not fallen behind with anything, he was still top of the class in all his subjects.

LIGHTS,

CAMERA,

ACTION!

Fast Fact!

Corbin was excellent at chemistry and loved doing lab experiments - he even won a special award for chemistry in his second year at high school. He was just like the brainiacs in High School Musical - however, he made sure he didn't stick with one group of people at school - he liked to be friends with everybody.

Trying times

Life might seem like plain sailing for Corbin Bleu, but this was not the case at all. For every audition where Corbin got the part, there were many others where he wasn't picked. Corbin had to come to terms with the reality that, at auditions, talent isn't enough – you have to look right for the part too. Corbin is mixed-race, and often casting directors were looking for people who were either entirely white or entirely black.

Corbin also struggled with the part he was given in his high school show during his second year. The show was the Eighties' musical *Footloose*. When Corbin auditioned, he never expected to be given the star part because, although he was a great actor and dancer, he wasn't as good as other people at singing. However, the lead role was exactly what he was given – the character of Ren, who not only has to be a dancing hotshot but who also has to sing some very difficult songs.

Corbin was immediately extremely worried about whether he could pull it off. The situation was made worse when some other kids, who were jealous of Corbin, started grumbling about how he shouldn't have been cast as Ren because his singing wasn't good enough. Corbin's teacher noticed that he seemed to be very stressed and reassured him that he could do it – his parents did the same.

So Corbin made up his mind to work extra-hard. He not only asked the musical director to stay late after each rehearsal so he could put in more practice, he also asked his parents to get him a vocal coach to help him with singing lessons at home. Corbin's dedication paid off. On opening night, he received a standing ovation. He also won one of the lead roles in the next school musical that same year, playing the part of Sonny in *Grease*.

Corbin had learned that you can't let nerves and difficult challenges hold you back.

Corbin's Top Tips

Corbin's parents always reminded him that acting is not about becoming rich and famous. A good actor always works hard, tries his best, and aims to create a performance he can be proud of – whether it's a small role in a school play or a lead part in a top TV drama.

Corbin The Star

A MUSICAL SENSATION

No one had any idea what a blockbusting success *High School Musical* was to become, turning Corbin and his co-stars into celebrities overnight.

Disney promoted *High School Musical* for several weeks before it was first shown on TV on 20 January 2006 – the movie's soundtrack was even released a week beforehand. But film bosses were still stunned by the number of viewers who tuned in to watch it – over seven million people! After airing on the Disney Channel for one month, viewing figures had risen to over twenty-six million – and they continued to grow.

In March, the movie soundtrack reached number one in the charts
– twice! It ended up being the biggest-selling album in the whole of 2006.
Six singles became gold discs by selling over 500,000 copies each.

Disney promoted a DVD and sing-along and dance-along versions of
the movie, which was shown all over the world, from Australia to the Middle
East, from South America to Africa. Corbin had become a worldwide sensation!

CORBIN
Quick Quiz

Q) Which scene did Corbin find the most
challenging in the movie?

A) The 'Get'cha Head in the Game'
routine – because he had to make handling a
basketball look effortless!

AWESOME AWARDS

Corbin was thrilled to find himself now attending prestigious award ceremonies.

High School Musical was nominated for six Emmy awards, winning two of them – for Outstanding Children's Programme and Outstanding Choreography. It also won the Television Critics Association Award for Outstanding Achievement in Children's Programming. And the cast won not just one but three Teen Choice Awards – for Choice Comedy/Musical, Best TV Chemistry (for Zac Efron and Vanessa Hudgens) and Choice Breakthrough Star (for Zac Efron).

Corbin wrote in his online journal at corbinbleu.com: 'All of us are so grateful for all of the success that High School Musical has achieved . . . That was my first time at the Emmys and to say that we actually won is mind-boggling to me.' At the Teen Choice Awards, he was highly excited to find that one of his idols, Johnny Depp, was accepting an award too.

Fast Fact!

Apart from the dance routines, Corbin's favourite scene in the movie is one where Chad is in the trophy room with Troy, trying to convince him not to go to callbacks for the musical, making him feel really guilty about letting the basketball team down. According to Corbin, it was the first time he'd been able to act being a bit of a bad guy.

Onwards and upwards

Corbin told thestarscoop.com: 'Disney is really great. Once you do one Disney thing, you're in their pack. You get to do a lot.' Next, he got to guest star on the premiere episode of the hit Disney TV show *Hannah Montana* with Miley Cyrus. Then, during the summer of 2006, Disney gave Corbin another great break: his first solo starring role in a movie. It was to be called *Jump In!* and was the story of a young boxer, Izzy Daniels (Corbin), who was following in the footsteps of his ex-boxer dad, trying to win the prestigious Golden Glove Award. But when Izzy's friend, Mary, convinces him to join a double-Dutch skipping tournament with her, he realises that he might actually be keener on the art of double-Dutching than boxing!

Fast Fact!

To get into shape for Jump In! Corbin trained at the Wild Card gym in Los Angeles with Bridgett 'Baby Doll' Riley, a boxer who had worked on other movies, such as Million Dollar Baby. Besides all the boxing training, he also had to perfect the skill of double-Dutching, and also various tricks to do while jumping the ropes, such as press-ups and splits. Phew!

Corbin was not only thrilled to be playing a solo lead for the first time, he was also highly delighted that his real dad was cast to play his dad in the movie. He wrote in his online journal at corbinbleu.com, 'Working with my dad was definitely one of the highlights of my career thus far.'

Corbin goes live

After landing a solo starring role in a movie, you might be wondering if there were any new challenges left for Corbin. The answer is yes: Corbin was about to branch out into music and become a recording artist!

Corbin had been asked to record a solo song for the soundtrack to *Jump In!* The song was called 'Push It to the Limit', and it was released in November 2006, before the movie soundtrack came out in January 2007. At the same time – from November 2006 to January 2007 – Corbin and the cast of *High School Musical* were on a live concert tour across America. For Corbin, acting, dancing and singing live was like revisiting the buzz and energy of his high school *Footloose* and *Grease* days, only on a scale a zillion times bigger and better! During the show, Corbin also performed his new single 'Push It to the Limit' and many fans

said that this was one of the very best parts of the concert. All Corbin's qualms about singing from earlier days had been well and truly put to rest. In fact, he was offered a recording contract to work on an individual album. Vanessa Hudgens and Ashley Tisdale were also given contracts to make their own albums, but record producers felt that Corbin was the only boy from *High School Musical* who truly had what it takes.

Fast Fact!

Prior to 'Push It to the Limit', the only time Corbin had recorded a solo song was a track called 'Circles' for Flight 29 Down. It was played as background music in an episode when Corbin's character was falling for a girl, but didn't know how to tell her.

Corbin the Pop Star

When Corbin started work on his solo album, he wrote in his online journal: 'It's so weird because the music industry is new territory for me. I've been singing for a long time, but never professionally. So I'm just giving it my all, hoping for the best, and singing my heart out.'

Corbin soon found himself thoroughly enjoying the experience. He likes a wide variety of music, from pop and hip-hop to R&B and soul, and he loved drawing on all these influences to come up with his own sound. Corbin thought it was like a mix of Usher and Justin Timberlake, with a bit of Alicia Keys thrown in, because he played piano on some tracks as well as singing.

Corbin called his album 'Another Side', because he felt he was developing another side to his talents, besides acting and dancing. It was released on 1 May 2007 in the United States and reached number 3 in the US Billboard 200. It sold about 18,000 copies in its first week! The album came out a month later in the United Kingdom. A reviewer wrote: 'His vocals, a pleasing mash of Michael Jackson and Jesse McCartney, make him a contender for a long-term career in music.'

Fast Fact!

Corbin especially loves his mum's favourite type of music: Eighties' pop. Maybe this is because it is so high-energy, just like Corbin himself.

★ CORBIN ★
Quick Quiz

Q) Who is Corbin's favourite rapper?

A) Kanye West

The Private Corbin

Corbin at home

Corbin's mum and dad have always reminded Corbin that acting is a job like any other job – what's important is how good you are at it, not fame and fortune. So at home, Corbin the star is treated just the same as all the other members of the family. If his mum or dad ask him to take his turn with the washing up, he has to get the rubber gloves on!

But Corbin wouldn't have things any other way. He loves living at home because the Reivers family are extremely close. For him, his family are all-important. Corbin loves and admires his parents greatly. He is extremely appreciative of all their support and invaluable advice over the years. Corbin would never dream of disrespecting his parents and he cannot understand anyone who does so.

Corbin is hugely proud of his three younger sisters. Hunter is just 4 years younger than him. When she was very little, she wanted to be just like Corbin. She did quite a lot of modelling and acting – but has more recently found that she loves sports and music more than show business. After Hunter, there is a big gap before Corbin's two youngest sisters – Phoenix is 12 years younger than Corbin, and Jag is 14 years younger. Corbin calls Phoenix 'mini-me' because she seems to be very like him in personality, whereas Jag seems to be more like Hunter.

Corbin Bleu ♡ X

Fast Fact!

Hunter started modelling even younger than Corbin - she appeared in an advert when she was only 3 months old!

Corbin at Work and Play

When Corbin is working, his days on set can be very long. He often has to be on the set of a TV show or a movie at 5.30 a.m. – yawn! Corbin doesn't mind though. He is highly professional and gives every job his all – besides, he doesn't think of work as work. He loves what he does, so for him, work is fun.

After a long day of filming, Corbin sits and plays the piano to relax, or mucks about with his three younger sisters or watches DVDs in his basement – perhaps with some mates. Corbin loves hanging out with his friends. They often go to a restaurant for a meal and they like to go to a bowling alley, ice rink or movie.

Who are Corbin's mates?

Corbin is a very outgoing, warm person who loves to be surrounded by mates. He finds it very easy to make friends. However, as all stars will tell you, one of the down-sides to being famous is that you can never be sure if new people you meet are interested in you for being you, or because you're a celebrity. Corbin feels happiest spending time with old mates he can really trust. He has become firm friends with his fellow cast-members on Flight 29 Down, High School Musical, Catch That Kid, Jump in! and Hannah Montana. Corbin also sees several old friends from high school and even two from as far back as primary school. He likes having a balance between showbiz friends and non-showbiz friends – it helps him to keep his feet on the ground and have time being just Corbin, rather than always feeling like Corbin the celeb.

Fast Fact!

Corbin's best birthday party was his 15th. He had 70 mates round to his house! They had a DJ and a pool table and video games playing on a big screen. Corbin knows that lots of young people in showbiz drink alcohol and do drugs, but he doesn't need things like these to have a great time.

ORK
EST
AY
ARDER

CORBIN
Quick Quiz

Q) What's Corbin's favourite way to spend an evening out?

A) To dance the night away at a club — as long as he doesn't have to get up early for work the next day!

Fast Fact!

Corbin has fave girl celebrities just like any regular teenage guy. He thinks Angelina Jolie and Jennifer Garner are especially gorgeous!

Corbin and lurve

According to lots of websites and magazines, Corbin is always falling in love with his co-stars. He has learned to laugh at such rumours, because they're just not true. Corbin has lots of friends who are girls, and he very much likes going on dates, but he doesn't have a serious girlfriend. He's always so busy going all over the place with his work that he can't be around a lot of the time – which he doesn't think would be fair on a girlfriend.

Corbin has said that if he was to have a steady girlfriend, she would have to be someone down-to-earth, like him. She'd have to be independent, with her own busy life, not just following him around all the time. He'd like to start off as friends first, and build a relationship slowly, so there'd be a deep bond of trust and honesty.

Is Corbin romantic? Well, he thinks so! He thinks it's important to do thoughtful old-fashioned things like hold the door open for a girl. He also likes to buy little presents like chocolates and roses. His idea of a perfect date would be a walk along the beach, under the stars, followed by a cosy dinner for two – and then dancing!

Dealing with fame

Since Corbin starred in High School Musical, young people all over the world recognise him. Wherever he goes, kids start calling his name and coming up to him to ask for an autograph or pose for a photo. Of course, Corbin was once a fan of famous actors himself – he remembers what this felt like, so he'll always go out of his way to talk to fans if he can. He loves making people happy like this. However, Corbin gets approached by so many people all the time that he can't always stop. If he did, he'd cause a crowd in no time – plus he'd never get anywhere! One of the problems is his trademark curly hair; he really stands out in a crowd – no one can possibly miss him!

Some of Corbin's faves

Favourite food: Corbin likes junk food like burgers and French fries! (He burns off all the calories with his dancing.) His favourite breakfast is pancakes and a chai latte from Coffee Bean.

Favourite TV show: The Amazing Race and Futurama.

Favourite movie: Corbin knows all the words and dance moves to The Rocky Horror Picture Show. He also loves the movie of the musical Chicago.

Favourite book: Corbin has always loved books. When he was little, his two favourite books were The True Story of the Three Little Pigs and The Stinky Cheese Man and Other Fairly Stupid Tales. Now Corbin reads everything from psychology textbooks to classic novels.

Favourite musician: Prince. Corbin has been to see him in concert twice.

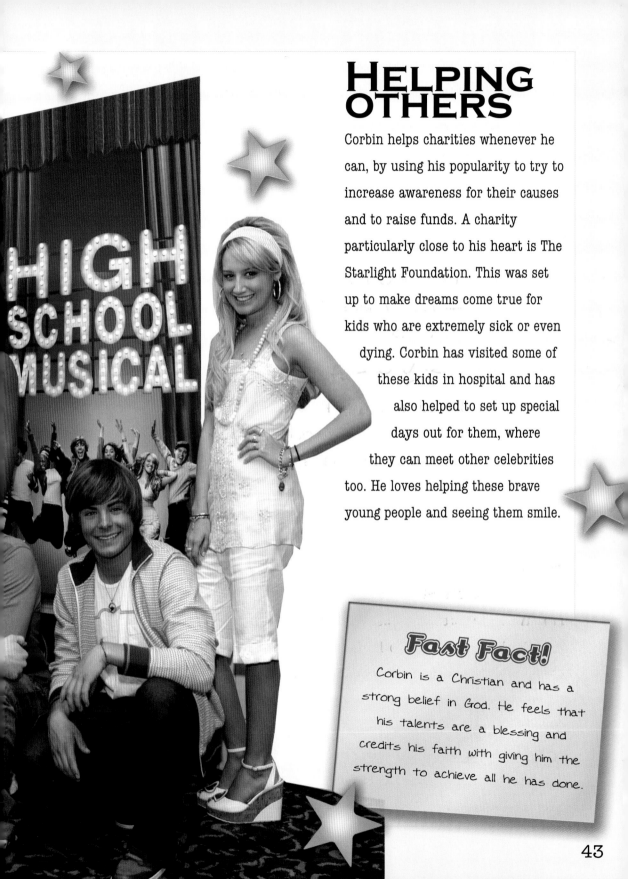

HELPING OTHERS

Corbin helps charities whenever he can, by using his popularity to try to increase awareness for their causes and to raise funds. A charity particularly close to his heart is The Starlight Foundation. This was set up to make dreams come true for kids who are extremely sick or even dying. Corbin has visited some of these kids in hospital and has also helped to set up special days out for them, where they can meet other celebrities too. He loves helping these brave young people and seeing them smile.

Fast Fact!

Corbin is a Christian and has a strong belief in God. He feels that his talents are a blessing and credits his faith with giving him the strength to achieve all he has done.

The Future's Bright for Corbin

The curtain falls on High School Musical

Corbin was delighted to reprise his role as Chad Danforth in two further High School Musical movies: *High School Musical 2: Sing It All or Nothing* and *High School Musical 3: Senior Year*. Corbin particularly loved HMS3, as his real-life dad once again played his on-screen dad, and he also got to perform a stunning junk-yard dance scene with one of his best friends, Zac Efron. Sadly, the magic of *High School Musical* could not go on for Corbin for ever, and this wonderful chapter in his life has now come to an end. So what lies ahead for this talented young star?

Making movies

In 2007, Corbin appeared in a movie version of *Flight 29 Down* called *The Hotel Tango* – and you'll continue to see Corbin starring on the big screen for a long time to come. He is determined to stretch himself as an actor and prove his talents by branching out into all sorts of films,

including horror, comedy, period drama and action. But Corbin also has his eye on getting into the action behind the scenes too. In 2008, he starred in a film about a young motocross racer, *Free Style*. Yet again, Corbin's dad played his on-screen dad – however Corbin and David not only acted in the film together, they co-produced the film too. Corbin has told *Time for Kids* that one of his goals is to become a great producer. 'I want to be able to control and have power over my own projects,' he has said. For the same reason, Corbin has set his sights on directing movies too – no doubt it's just a matter of time before he's sitting in the director's chair!

Making music

Corbin has become just as passionate about singing and songwriting, as he is about dancing. After performing in a sell-out tour of concert dates across America in summer 2008, he set straight to work on an album of brand new material. As well as developing his career as a recording artist, Corbin would also love to show his singing and dancing talents in the theatre – one of his greatest dreams is to return to his childhood home, New York, as the star of a musical on Broadway.

Back to school?

While Corbin was still in high school, he became very interested in medicine and considered becoming a doctor rather than an actor. He even went to a week-long course at John Hopkins University in Baltimore, USA, for young students who were thinking about training in medicine. However, upon graduating from high school, Corbin had to make the difficult decision to put off going to college. Despite being accepted into Stanford University, he chose to follow his heart and concentrate on his acting, singing and dancing career, making the most of all the fantastic showbiz opportunities that were coming his way. But because Corbin loves learning, he may one day still study for a university degree. As an actor, he has always been interested in what makes different people tick – he has said that, besides medicine, he would really enjoy studying psychology.

Corbin's Top Tips

Corbin believes that doing your best in your education is very important – not just so you can have a good choice of careers, but also to develop yourself as as a knowledgeable, interesting person.

Personal plans

Apart from performing, the main love in Corbin's life is his big, close family. He definitely plans on getting married one day and having kids – he wants several of them. He doesn't want to wait too long either – he'd like to be a young dad with lots of energy. Not that having lots of energy has ever been a problem for him! He's clearly got all the the buzz, talent and drive he needs to blaze a trail along all the many exciting new directions which lie ahead. Watch out world, here comes Corbin Bleu!